Answers to Questions I Didn't Know I Needed to Ask:

A Guide for Anyone Who Works With Children and Adolescents

Suzanne E. Donovan, EdD

Table of Contents

Forward

The effects of adverse childhood experiences (ACEs) often manifest themselves in children whose behavior is unpredictable, adolescents demonstrating risky behaviors, and adults who face serious medical, mental, and economic challenges. A common reaction to this can be "what's wrong with you?". With an understanding of ACEs and their effects comes a better question which should be "what happened to you?".

The purpose of this book is to inform anyone who may be interested in the alarming preponderance of adverse childhood experiences, better known as ACEs. Since 1995 psychologists have studied the effects of ACEs on the present and future health of children as they grow into adulthood. Some are asking "why am I just hearing about this?". Dr. Nadine Burke Harris is one of the people asking this question. In her book, *Healing the Long-Term Effects of Childhood Adversity,* she states:

> "Along with my excitement at finding the ACE Study's demonstration of links between adversity and disease came a wave of indignation: *Why was I only hearing about this now?* This study was clearly a game-changer, yet I hadn't learned about it in med school, public-health

school, or even residency. Felitti and Anda published their initial ACE findings in 1998, and I didn't read them until 2008. Ten Years!" (Harris, 2018)

This author echoes Dr. Harris's words. I have been fortunate to learn of these research projects and their astonishing findings. Therefore, it is my intention to bring together these findings and forward this research and information on to others to use in their classrooms, clinical practice, or in their community outreach work with both children and adults.

Moving from: *"What's wrong with you?"* To: *"What happened to you?"*

Trauma affects the ability of young children to learn and the future health of adolescents as they reach adulthood. We modify our approaches to children and youth with Trauma-Informed Care to compensate for childhood trauma.

Scenario #1:

Billy Age 10:

Billy entered the classroom every day with an attitude of "I'll get you before you can get me". He spent most of each day in solitude, away from the other students. His combative attitude was less evident when he was working closely with a teacher or aid. Billy was seeking an attachment to a replacement caregiver. Investigation showed that he was being bullied at home by an older brother while his parents were at work. This physical abuse coupled with parental neglect, even if it was unintentional, was victimizing Billy. Once a conference was held and the parents were advised of the problem, it could be resolved. Unfortunately, he did not live into adulthood. He died of a substance abuse overdose or suicide while in his teens. He was a victim of both bullying and neglect, in an affluent home. ACEs are at times unintentional and can happen in the best of circumstances.

"Childhood experiences...create the person. These organizing childhood experiences can be consistent, nurturing, structured and enriched, resulting in flexible, responsible, empathetic and creative adults. Conversely, neglect, chaos, violence and threat create impulsive, aggressive, remorseless and antisocial individuals. An appreciation of biological relativity and the crucial organizing power of childhood experience have never been more important in our species." (Perry, 2013)

Children are quite often subjects of abuse, intentional (physical or emotional) or accidental (natural disasters or weather-related occurrences) that form the adult that they may become in later years. As Dr. Perry states, if the child develops in a caring environment, he more than likely will grow to be a caring and responsible adult. The child whose brain organizes as his age increases, with the ability to move, think, connect with others, speak, plan and with a sense of belonging developing as he grows, will enter adulthood free or at least with fewer trauma related experiences. Youth entering adulthood, age 17-18 years old, having experienced trauma-related experiences, may have disruptions in a healthy adult lifestyle. Children who have had adverse childhood experiences may fall victim to many health issues as adults such as heart problems, diabetes, obesity, cancer, substance abuse and the list goes on, including early mortality, ten to twenty (10-20) years prior to the expected age. As these young adults age, they may have difficulty regulating their behavior and emotions, relating their behavior to their emotions and thoughts, and attaching reasoning as to why they behave and think as they do. Without the ability to perform the following operations, regulate, relate, and reason, the child, and then the adolescent, is unable to get past the negative experiences he has had. He is unable to develop the ability to build resilience, the ability to get past his exposure to adversity, as he ages. In addition to the person developing, the growing child may pass this inability to develop to his family, creating an inter-generational problem. This inter-generational issue has been discovered in much of the research.

The traumatized child may also demonstrate developmental differences from his untraumatized peers. Traumatized children may sense a chronic threat of danger causing constant hyperarousal. They may not be able to regulate their emotions, causing them to develop mental health issues later in life and experience differences in executive functioning. This may lead to mood disorders such as dysphoria later as an adult. Children able to learn coping skills and regulate their emotions can build relationships easier and have more satisfying social connections with their peers. Children who have been traumatized may experience diminished social reward for activities. They are missing the motivation to connect with others and to gain pleasure from the experience. This is the child who is becoming socially distanced, self-isolated, from his peers. Resilience for this child will include becoming more socially connected with others both in his age group and outside. Difficulty with executive functioning, reacting to the real world, can result in difficulty processing social information, cognition, and behavioral control later in life. Finally, children may overreact to perceived threats and stimuli, developing a "threat" bias. Anxiety disorders can develop over time. Some of the outcomes from developmental issues could be black and white thinking (no grey areas), taking things out of proportion (everything is either all or nothing), focusing on the negative (I am all bad, no redeeming qualities), predicting disaster (nothing good can happen), global decisions (no middle area), or unrealistic ideas (I am able to do impossible things). All of these are distorted realities for the traumatized child.

Trauma and the Child

Scenario #2:

Patty

Patty had a negative attitude about school. She had been in enough trouble both in and out of school to have been incarcerated briefly. Every time she returned to school, she attacked a smaller child and had to be returned to police custody. Her only "safe" place was within the juvenile justice system. In a detention center she was safe from all types of abuse, household challenges, and neglect. She was fed, had clean clothes and had a bed. Most of all, she could demand respect from the other inmates because of the reputation she had developed. Patty was the victim of home abuse, neglect, and a witness to severe abuse and fighting. As she aged out of the juvenile system she fell into the adult justice system. The traumas she experienced as a child followed her and exacerbated her behaviors. As an adult, she is still incarcerated.

Defining trauma helps to explain all the adverse experiences included in ACEs. The following definition is a compilation of definitions from a variety of sources.

Trauma is an event that causes the inability to mentally or emotionally deal with reality after a stimulus or an event that was unexpected, accidental, physical or natural, perpetrated on someone, or in the presence of a witness.

Trauma can be mentally or emotionally disabling leaving the person unable to see the real world as it is. The stimulus can be real or imagined and usually comes when least expected. It can come from an accident, a purposeful occurrence or a naturally occurring situation. It can come from the effects of a severe winter storm or the bully on the playground. The customary response is usually flight, fight, or in some instances freeze. The victim can either remove themselves from the situation, if possible, physically defend himself, or, in many cases, freeze. Many times, children run away when faced with a challenging home situation. Other times they fight, either with siblings, schoolmates, or others. Freeze has recently been added to the fight/flight response as people often find themselves frozen with fear in one of these situations. We have often heard someone say that the reason they were assaulted was that they were too afraid to fight or run. This can be true, especially for a child. For the child, the response can affect him for life when this trauma is a result of adverse childhood experiences throughout his lifetime. All of the ACEs are traumatic events that continue to affect the healthy body and mind of the individual child.

Imagine the child who is repeatedly assaulted in his home by an older person. If he is too young to run, he may continually hide or physically distance himself from this person or others until he is old enough to run away. Once away from his home, he may seek refuge with others, but these may not be the most reliable people. An older adolescent may choose to fight it out with the perpetrator or get consolation from illegal drugs or other unhealthy or risky activities. The child of any age who constantly witnesses parental abuse may choose to defend the victimized parent at the risk of his own safety. Sometimes even the placement outside the family home is not a safe place and children run from these homes or begin to be aggressive toward other children in the house. Freezing with fear or out of distress can cause physical reactions for a child. Crying, complaints of stomach aches, and issues such as encopresis or enuresis can occur further causing the child embarrassment and fear. (Diagnostic and Statistical Manual of Mental Disorders, DSM-5-TR) All contribute to the need for the child to want to run, become combative or hide from the situation. Even school may no longer be a "safe place" or the sanctuary it should be and the child continues his combative behavior to his school mates and other school staff. Fight, flight, or freeze becomes all the child is able to do in traumatic situations. It becomes his customary behavior in all situations. He no longer has confidence in himself or anyone else to help manage his behavior and emotions in these situations.

When looking at trauma and the effect it has on children, a closer look at the neurological capabilities of the child is necessary. Children perceive things very differently from adults. Where an adult may see an argument between partners as a minor event, the child observing this event may see it as a threat to both the partners and himself, therefore expanding the trauma to something that will be a lasting memory. When a parent uses a slap or another physical punishment, he may be doing this because this is what was done to him as a child. The parent sees this as the correct manner of punishing the child. This is where inter-generational trauma occurs, but the child does not see it this way. The child's perception is only what is directly happening to him. Understanding what the action is does not always become clear to the child as it does to an adult. Looking at perception as a psychological study, it is obvious that perception is in the eye of the individual. Perception is also important to resilience, to determine if the experience is traumatizing or may be a learning one. For each individual, what he sees is unique to him, like a picture or some kind of illustration would be. Optical illusions can be seen clearly by most adults, but the child does not have the ability to distinguish between real and illusionary. When this theory is applied to trauma, it becomes clear why the child looks at trauma and becomes fearful. For the child everything is real, to be feared and presents as a lasting memory. Another example is what the child sees on the news on television. Is it the same as the video game being played in his home or is it real? When the child sees a military conflict on television is it comparable to the video game his older siblings play? The young child does not have the neurological development to be able to distinguish between a game and reality. The child resorts to perception, he determines it is what he sees. The child's brain should be organizing according to his chronological age helping him to reason. The child who is traumatized will not have the neurological development that is needed to organize and reason as a child living in a safe environment. Nor will he be able to distinguish between what is real and what is a false perception. Perception is important to resilience as well, to determine if the experience is in fact traumatic or a learning one for the child. Regulating, relating, and reasoning may not work in the child's brain yet. The delay in this ability to perceive is caused by trauma in the case of Adverse Childhood Experiences (ACEs), and by the age of the child in normal situations. The speech and language learning that should develop between six (6) and twelve (12) months, may be delayed; and the ability to distinguish between angry or fearful facial expressions may not be evidenced at the seven (7) month mark. Where the child should be able to see a salient threat of possible intentional danger, he may not see that it is directed at him. Failure to understand when a threat is directed at him will become an adverse experience.

In addition to neurological health issues, economic issues arise. Children who have been subjected to adverse experiences may be deprived of appropriate education and interruption of the development of his brain, creating the issue of poverty due to the inability to join the work force as a young adult. This has now become a multi-generational issue. Issues of food insecurity and homelessness reach all generations living together. Homelessness and poverty cause anxiety for adults, subsequently causing anger and physical retaliation on children. Addiction and illegal drug use complicates the problem. What we call "household challenges" can make even going to school difficult for the traumatized child. He sees interactions in the classroom as negative and threatening, especially when real or perceived bullying occurs. He may go from one extreme to the other, socially isolating or becoming physically aggressive.

Research on social isolation and loneliness by Dr. Julianne Holt-Lundstad and Dr. Vivek Murthy (United States Surgeon General, 12/2014 to 4/2017 and 3/2023 to present) reported in Dr. Murthy's book, *Together*, have brought another social issue to the forefront. (Murthy, 2020) Research has shown that there is a correlation between social isolation and adult mental and medical diseases. Since there has been found to be a correlation between ACEs and adult mental, medical, and addiction disabilities, the assumption can be made that there is a correlation between ACEs and social isolation. Children who have experienced trauma also experience social isolation. Looking at examples of children, particularly the ones in the scenarios at the end of this book, they all appear to be experiencing some kind of social isolation, whether self-imposed or imposed intentionally by someone else.

Dr. John Cacioppo in Dr. Murthy's book *Together* states that personal relationships get "under the skin" and that social isolation disrupts perception, behavior, and physiology, leading to an early death, just as adverse experiences can cause death ten (10) to twenty (20) years sooner than expected in actuarial tables. (Murthy, 2020) Sudden loss of a loved one can result in "takotsubo", a Japanese word meaning "broken heart syndrome". For the adult who has been subjected to adverse experiences this adds to the already disrupted life. Losing a loved one can cause greater isolation and a negative perception of self. The already low self-esteem and

self-value continues to diminish. According to both Murthy and Cacioppo,

the Pandemic of 2020 has caused many situations where social isolation

and loneliness has caused severe illness and the associated early death.

(Murthy, 2020)

Treatment

Scenario #3

13-year-old: Mary

Mary came into school each day with a positive attitude, but as the day went on her behavior deteriorated. A Formative Evaluation program was instituted. The following was observed: Period 1 was English where she functioned well. Period 2 was a hands-on Science class where all went well. Period 3 was Social Studies, also a success. Period 4 began as she walked down the hall, refusing to enter the classroom. Once in the room, she made loud noises, threw books, and made a general disturbance. She was behind in her understanding of mathematics and as such it was better to be labeled bad than dumb. A tutor helped her get up to speed and get the situation resolved. She was growing up in a household where education was not perceived as important and her family income was below the poverty level. There was also evidence of drug abuse. Many ACEs were evident in this family in addition to low income and lack of regard for education. Mary saw much violence around her in her household. Her brothers were combative as were her parents. Although getting an education and being able to remove herself from the situation, she was a victim of ACEs from each of the 3 categories. Mary grew to follow the pattern she was raised in, a minimum wage job and living along the fringes of poverty.

Looking at ACEs and their impact on children, the first question that arises

is how to treat children who have already been exposed to this difficult

situation. The Center for the Developing Child at Harvard University found that two-thirds (2/3) of the United States population they studied reported

one (1) ACE and one-fourth (1/4) of the population reported three (3) or

more. Taking into consideration the numbers of effected individuals,

Trauma-informed care has become a method to serve as an aid in the

treatment for adverse experiences for children. Reducing the need for

treatment of the stress caused by adverse experiences can come from

providing services that are supportive of both the individual and family's

needs, through community services. The National Scientific Council on the

Developing Child first used the term "toxic stress" in the early 2000's to

identify the effects of ACEs on the brain of the growing child. Adding "toxic"

to the stress emphasizes the critical nature of the need for immediate

treatment. All of the ACEs, including neighborhood violence, racism,

migrant issues and poverty are included as toxic stressors. Racism and

neighborhood violence need to be controlled before children can be free

from the negative influences of ACEs. Children entering the United States

as migrants need support with food and living security and assistance with language barriers. These children have already faced many or all of the ACEs. in their journey into the United States.

As children age, following their health scenarios to watch for debilitating illness is necessary. Watching for signs of the results of childhood abuse and helping caregivers to work with youth in treatment will assist in keeping illness from becoming fatal and these same subjects from making poor choices in activities and having unfortunate consequences.

The second issue is to determine how to begin to prevent adverse experiences from happening to children and prevent toxic stress. Looking primarily at developing a safe, supportive community in which a child will live and thrive and the building of resilience in the child appear to be the initial steps. Studying results from the Sanctuary Institute studies, developing a safe school environment for children who are subjects of childhood trauma is critical. Dr. Sandra Bloom and her colleagues developed a trauma-informed facility in Philadelphia in the late 1980's. The purpose of this facility was to provide clinical and organizational changes to support safety and recovery for children and adolescents who were being victimized by traumatic experiences, using trauma-informed strategies. Removing stress, racism, and violence can start to rid the environment of community discord through which ACEs develop. Assistance with education for adults in need of training of some sort to acquire employment, reduce poverty and homelessness as well as other issues, can reduce some of the causes of abuse and other ACEs, particularly household challenges. Supporting community programs to educate caregivers for employment and childcare can reduce toxic stress for the adults in targeted neighborhoods. Additional programs to support communities plagued by racism and neighborhood violence can come from support groups like churches, other houses of worship, schools and community centers. Racism is not only a Black and White issue but can be categorized in other combinations of groups of people. A good definition could be *A learned automatic negative reaction to a person solely based on the ethnic group to which they belong.* "Learned" is the key word as this issue becomes inter-generational as groups become aggressive in defending their neighborhoods. Working with communities to reduce racism and the resultant violence is certainly a concrete step to reducing neighborhood discord and therefore the resulting ACEs effecting children. ACEs has become a social problem and a public health problem according to some, not only effecting inner city neighborhoods, but all types of cities and towns in the United States.

Background of Studies of Childhood Trauma

Prior to the Adverse Childhood Experience study by Felitti and Anda in 1995, several psychologists studied the health and behavior of children and adults. In 1998, a developmental psychologist, Dr. Emmy Warner published the results of her three decades of research on six hundred and ninety-eight (698) children born in Hawai'i in 1955. Two-thirds (2/3) of the children were from stable environments, while the remaining one-third (1/3) came from more unstable homes, deeming them "at-risk". "At-risk students often lack ownership of school activities and basic skills...lack self-confidence, have home problems and encounter indifference from their teachers." (Donovan, 1998) All of the above would characterize a child who had been traumatized, a victim of ACEs. Of the "at-risk" group, two out of every three registered mild to severe behavioral and mental health problems. The last one (1) out of three (3) were able to demonstrate academic and social success. As these children grew into adults, some who were not particularly talented did not allow their circumstances to affect achievement. (Konnikova, 2016) Warner also found that the children who were originally "at-risk" overcame low expectations, they were active and sociable as opposed to withdrawn and socially isolated. Part of the difference was that they had at least one role model who supported them as opposed to caregivers who were negligent and abusive. They developed at least one work skill that reinforced their self-worth and created their place in their peer group as opposed to being abused, neglected, ostracized and possibly unemployed. All of these become buffers for the adverse effects of children's experiences. (Center for Resilient Children) Werner's study would become a precursor to ACEs.

In 1999, Dr. Norman Garmezy released a report from four (4) decades of research (from the early 1950's) with thousands of children looking at their ability to overcome adversity or trauma. Garmezy noticed that how well children overcame aversity depended on the type and intensity of the trauma they underwent. Chronic adversity has a cumulative and repeated effect on the individual. Garmezy determined that trauma inflicted on a child by a parent usually fell into this chronic realm, whereas witnessing a traumatic event may not have had as much of an overall effect. (Konnikova, 2016)

Dr. George Bonanno has been studying the differences in how certain people can deal with adversity and some do not. In his twenty-five (25) year study, he found that the majority of his study subjects were good at dealing with stress caused by trauma. The answer he came up with relatively often was that it was the person's conception of the event. Whether the event is perceived as traumatic or not is in the person's perception of the event. Bonanno coined the phrase "potentially traumatic event" or PTE, to explain what he means by perception or conception. The focus of his research has been narrowed to the study of serious harm through acute negative events. In his epidemiological study of traumatic events, his data shows that trauma does not necessarily predict "later functioning", only if there is a negative response by the person being abused. In terms of ACEs, the adversity is usually traumatizing. As human beings, we can make more of an incident than what may be obvious. We worry or exaggerate the stressor until we have blown it completely out of proportion. All of these studies have the feel of a version of the results of Adverse Childhood

Experiences (ACEs) research. (Konnikova, 2016)

To look into treatment for those who have had these negative experiences

and to establish prevention theories for the initial onset of this social issue,

the following will look at into the research done in two (2) separate studies

of ACEs (Adverse Childhood Experiences), the California study, 1995-1997

and the Appalachian study, 2018.

The Beginning of Kaiser-Permanente's ACEs Research

As a precursor to the Adverse Childhood Experience study, in 1985 Dr. Vincent Felitti noticed a trend with the progress of the patients in his obesity clinic study. (Kain and Terrell, 2018) His patients demonstrating the most success with the obesity program, were prematurely dropping out of the program prior to completion, only to regain the lost weight. After interviewing three hundred (300) of the patients who had dropped out, he discovered that they all had something in common, what is now called adverse childhood experiences (ACEs). This study of Dr. Felitti's became the start of the first public health study looking into childhood trauma.

To complete the group of study researchers, Dr. Felitti included Dr. Robert Anda an epidemiologist at the Center for Disease Control and Prevention who had been studying the correlation between adults and their behavioral health and the cardiovascular disease they reported to their doctors. The first Adverse Childhood Experiences (ACEs) study took place from 1995-1997 in Southern California (Kaiser-Permanente Research and The Center for Disease Control and Prevention Research) This research focused on three (3) things: childhood abuse, adolescent risk behaviors and adult health. Kaiser-Permanente had a client list of over forty-five thousand (45,000) members from which seventeen-thousand four hundred twenty-one (17,421) were selected. (Harris, 2018) The selected group were both men and women, (primarily White 74.8%) enrolled in The Health Maintenance Organization program. (Kaiser Permanente) While being given annual physical examinations the group was also given surveys concerning their childhood experiences. Data were collected from the approximately seventeen thousand (17,000) members of this health organization in two (2) waves and the results of the data from the health examination and ACEs questionnaire were correlated. This initial ACEs research project was deemed the most important epidemiology study in the last fifty plus (50+) years. (Perry, 2021) In 2007, Dr. Anda created the ACE Score Calculator to provide clinicians with numerical scores to evaluate subjects and their ACE scores. (Kain and Terrell, 2018)

According to the American Journal of Preventative Medicine, this study was the first of its kind attempting to correlate childhood experiences and health issues later in adult life. Further, it has been determined that health, including morbidity and mortality, and early childhood traumas have a close correlation. This long-term relationship can be the cause of many public health problems. Holmes defines maltreatment of children as any kind of abuse or neglect of a child less than eighteen (18) years of age by an older adult. Signs of this abuse can be physical such as bruising or broken limbs or behavioral, aggression or social withdrawal. Issues with eating or appropriate choice of clothing (summer weight clothing in winter or winter clothing in summer) can also be evident. (Holmes, 2021)

Demographics for the population of this initial study

The ratio of gender was close to being evenly spread, fifty-four percent (54%) Male; forty-six percent (46%) Female. Ethnicity was primarily Caucasian, seventy-four-point eight percent (74.8%); Black, seven-point two percent (7.2%); Asian/Pacific Islander, eleven-point two percent (11.2%)

and Other, two-point three percent (2.3%). A plurality of forty-six-point

four percent (46.4%), were over the age of sixty (60). In addition, other age

groups were widely spread, percentages of participants increasing with age,

ages nineteen to twenty-nine (19-29), five-point three percent (5.3%);

thirty to thirty-nine (30-39), nine-point eight percent (9.8%); forty to forty-

nine (40-49), eighteen-point six percent (18.6%); and fifty to fifty-nine (50-

59) nineteen-point nine percent (19.9%). Educational levels of participants

increased with age as well, of the participants thirty-nine point three

(39.3%) had an undergraduate college degree or higher, thirty-five-point

nine percent (35.9%) had some college experience, seventeen point six

(17.6%) had high school diplomas and a minority, seven-point two percent

(7.2%), were not high school graduates. It is not surprising that the study

was comprised of educated, upper- and middle-class white individuals as

this was the composition of the Kaiser Permanente health group in

Southern California. (Harris, 2018)

In some categories one gender or the other reported a greater percentage

of positive responses to the questions. Other categories, such as violence, were relatively equal in responses. The higher percentages of prevalence of ACEs by survey category were as follows:

Abuse

Twenty-seven percent (27%) of women and (twenty-nine-point nine percent (29.9%) of the men reported physical abuse; twenty-four-point seven percent (24.7%) of women reported sexual abuse. Totals of men and women reported the following by category: ten-point six percent (10.6%) Emotional Abuse; twenty-eight-point three percent (28.3%) Physical Abuse; and twenty-point seven percent (20.7%) Sexual Abuse.

Household Challenges

Of women twenty-nine-point five percent (29.5%) and twenty-three-point eight percent (23.8%) of men reported Substance Abuse; Violence on Mother was reported by twelve-point seven percent (12.7%) of the total participants. Mental Illness was reported by twenty-three-point three percent (23.3%) of women participants. Parental Separation or Divorce was reported by twenty-four-point five percent (24.5%) of women.

Neglect

Fourteen-point eight percent (14.8%) of all participants reported Emotional neglect and nine-point percent (9.9%) Physical neglect.

Score Prevalence by gender and number of experiences showed thirty-four-point five percent (34.5%) of women reported zero (0) ACEs and twenty-four-point five percent (24.5%) reported one (1) ACE. Thirty-eight-point eight percent (38%) of men reported zero (0) ACEs and twenty-seven-point nine percent (27.9%) reported one (1) ACE. Close to sixty-six percent (66%) of respondents reported one (1) ACE and greater than twenty percent (20%) reported three (3) or more. Of the women respondents, fifteen-point two percent (15.2%) reported four (4) or more ACEs and nine-point two (9.2 %) of men reported four (4) or more ACEs.

Social and economic conditions related to the community environment around the respondents made some groups of respondents more vulnerable to experiencing adverse childhood experiences. ACE scores were calculated for a total sum of all categories. A correlation demonstrated that the greater the number of ACEs during childhood the greater the risk for negative health outcomes for adults. (CDC and Kaiser Permanente, 2016)

The First Adverse Childhood Experience Questionnaire

The following ACEs questionnaire items refer to events or experiences perpetrated in the presence of or to the child. The following ten (10) research survey items, relating to a child aged zero (0) to eighteen (18) years of life, were used in the initial Kaiser-Permanente CDC ACEs study.

Abuse

Emotional Abuse

An older family member (for instance a parent, stepparent, grandparent or older sibling) uses loud, abusive, threatening, profane or any kind of language that makes the child fear for his/her safety. This abuse can also include belittling and degrading the child. This child never seems to hear a good word about himself, his appearance or behavior. The self-esteem of the child continually diminishes. Even if the child does not understand the meaning of the word, his self-esteem is lost.

Physical Abuse

An older family member (as above) throws, hits, slaps, grabs, or pushes the child, leaving physical marks and fear of further violence. This abuse can be inter-generational as a result of the perpetrator having been traumatized as a child himself. Sometimes abuse to an infant is referred to as Shaken Baby Syndrome with trauma continuing to younger children. This is not accidental but is purposeful and continues over time. In situations where the child seeks help from an adult, neglect will be evidenced as there could also be an absence of touching or comforting when the child is confronted in this aggressive manner by another family member or even a stranger.

Sexual Abuse

An older person (at least 5 years older) makes physical/sexual contact with the child in ways that make the child uncomfortable. Notice "uncomfortable" as this can be physical contact or nonphysical but humiliating including photographing. Both boys and girls can be victimized in this way. Sexual abuse can continue over a long period of time when the child is afraid to talk about this abuse. Children are often told not to talk about the abuse as they will be considered bad, putting the onus on the victim, the child. This may be a family member or stranger perpetrating the abuse.

Household Challenges

Mother is treated violently.

Violence in the home by a male, boyfriend, husband, or other male causing harm or physical injury to a female caretaker using fists or weapons. There have been incidents of this also happening to a father or father-figure by an abusive female. Men who have been taught not to hit women can be victimized and become susceptible to this kind of violence in front of a child.

Substance Abuse

Household member is using illegal drugs, prescription drugs illegally or abusing alcohol. Children who live with substance and alcohol abuse live in a state of fear. The constant state of not knowing the effect of the drug on the family member will keep children in this situation anxious and fearful. Adults using excessive alcohol and prescription, or illegal drugs are unpredictable, leaving family members unaware of what to expect from this family member when he/she returns to the residence.

Mental Illness

Household member who is mentally ill, depressed or has attempted suicide. Mental illness can range from anxiety to severe depression and if not treated can reflect on the treatment of family members. Add to this the horror of witnessing a suicide for the child by the family member who falls into any of these categories. Instability in the financial situation of the family can also be a result of mental illness when family finances are used for purchase of illegal drugs. Substance abuse of legal and illegal drugs can be a result of mental illness.

Separation/divorce

Parents separated or divorced leaving a full-time single-parent household. A parent leaving causes feelings of abandonment for the child and a large burden for both parenting obligations and financially for the remaining parent. Anger, frustration, and financial insecurity are a result. Where there was once a housing and a food secure home now there is uncertainty about these necessities for all family members remaining.

Incarceration

One or both parents are incarcerated leaving a single-parent or non-parental caregiver. When one or both parents are out of the home for an extended period of time, the family income is certainly in jeopardy. The child also loses his connection with the incarcerated parent when he no longer has the opportunity to make visits with the missing parent, particularly when the incarcerated parent is in a distant facility.

Neglect

Emotional

"Just-not-there" or lacking supportive attachment. These parent(s) are not attentive or supportive. Family members are not connected or supportive of one another. Feelings of loneliness keep the child from functioning normally. In some instances, the caregiver does not support school attendance, further separating the child from friends and other people in general who may have become his support system. A younger child could also be left at home to care for himself or left in the care of a slightly older child to care for other siblings while parent(s) work or are involved in other activities, leaving the child in a situation he is not mature enough to handle. This leaves the child with feelings of not being valued.

Physical

Not providing regular meals or having clean clothes. Lack of support for school attendance and activities. There is no adult supervision. The family lives in poverty and possibly homelessness and there is food uncertainty, a reasonable concern about there being the meals most children take for granted.

These ten (10) questions were given to the adults being treated in the Kaiser-Permanente program. Even though most of the study participants were middle to upper class, they all had a number of ACEs in common and evidence of resulting health problems. A very different population of participants were surveyed in the 2018 Appalachian ACEs study.

The Appalachian ACE Study

A 2018 report of ACEs research, *Exploring Adverse Childhood Experiences in Appalachia,* revealed the results of the beginning of a longitudinal study of ACEs as it applies to residents in this geographic area of the United States. The study was done by Oak Ridge Associated Universities and the Center for Disease Control's (CDC) Division of Violence Prevention. This study was based on the preponderance of overdosing of Opioids and rising resultant mortality rate in twenty-five (25) to forty-four (44) year-olds. This group of adults were experiencing over seventy percent (70%) more opioid deaths than the remainder of the United States. This pioneering study of ACEs

began in 2017 to better understand the effect of ACEs on children in that

specific area of the United States. Since some of the ACEs that children in

Appalachia were experiencing were missing from the first study, the

following were added by ORAU and the CDC.

These additional ten (10) adversities witnessed or experienced by a child

were added, bringing the total of survey items to twenty (20). With news

broadcasts as graphic and constantly on the television screen, the following

incidents can be witnessed by a child from any distance and at any time.

Adding these ten (10) experiences to the survey can change the scores of

answers to the research questionnaire dramatically. Some of the following

ACE additions have proven to be very disturbing to view or experience. It is

obvious from the additional questions that the focus of the Appalachian

ACEs study is on these particular areas of the United States.

The second set of ten (10) in the ACE Questionnaire:

Natural Disasters such as severe storms, tornadoes, hurricanes, and floods. The resultant loss of homes for people in these storm-ravaged areas caused homelessness, loss of employment, food insecurity, and poverty. According to the National Weather Service, in 2021, ninety-seven (97) natural disasters occurred in the United States, sixty-four (64) severe thunderstorms, fourteen (14) wildfires, heat waves, droughts and twelve (12) winter storms. All of these affecting the lives of countless young children in addition to their adult caregivers.

War torn areas of the world and **refugee experiences**, such as the United States border issue, the 2022 start of the war in Ukraine and the civil unrest in the Middle East. **Mass murders and terrorism** were experienced or graphically displayed on television screens. Mass murders appear to be occurring on an almost daily basis, with children and adults dying in front of the American people on television every night. In the year 2021 in the United States, six hundred, ninety-three (693) mass shootings (four (4) or more victims with each shooting) occurred, killing seven hundred three (703) and injuring two thousand eight hundred forty-two (2842). Forty-four thousand (44,000) people died of gun violence. (Wikipedia, Mass Shootings in the United States) In 2022, there were six hundred forty-seven (647) mass shootings and forty-five thousand, ten (45,010) people died of gun violence. (Gun Violence Archive) During the first half of 2023, over four hundred (420) mass shootings occurred, more than two (2) per day leaving four-hundred-fifty (450) dead and one-thousand-seventy-five (1775) injured. (CNN Aug. 5, 2023)

Community gang violence and school violence is witnessed or experienced. Shootings are occurring in neighborhoods in front of or to school children. These same children see police officers in their schools daily. Add to this the experience of bomb threats in their schools, causing fear of the very place many children look to as a safe place of sanctuary. Schools are expected by students to be places that provide a safe environment for healing and protection. According to *Education Week*, in 2022 there were fifty-one (51) school shootings, both elementary and high schools, making this virtually a weekly occurrence. Thirty-two (32) students and eight (8) adults were killed, one hundred (100) were injured. This is the most school shootings in one year since *Education Week* began tracking in 2018.

Bullying toward the child or witnessing others being bullied. Bullying has almost become a common place thing in our schools and on our playgrounds. In addition to physical bullying, cyber bullying has been a silent epidemic, affecting numerous school students, leaving emotional bruising in place of physical scars. Even if the child is not himself being bullied, he is a victim of the bully in fear for his own safety when he sees his friends being bullied.

Death of attachment-figure such as head-of-household or caretaker. This can be particularly distressing when the death takes place in the workplace or as a violent accident. The suddenness of an event like this can catch a child unaware and cause the freeze effect.

Drug overdose or Job-related accident of attachment-figure. Child witnessing a drug overdose of a family or household member. (A direct happening as a result of the existing opioid epidemic as in Appalachia.)

Once again, the suddenness of this event can cause the flight/fight/freeze response.

Homelessness, Displacement, Parental unemployment, lack of community resources and food insecurity. Food insecurity particularly affects children who live in situations where there is no guarantee where or if there will be a meal coming. This is most distressing during school holiday breaks and summer vacation when there are no school or federally funded meals available. Economic decline caused by fewer jobs creates increased stress and a sense of hopelessness.

Multiple divorces, changes in adults within the household, additions of step and half siblings into the household, and constant changing of the family configuration causes instability for the child.

In 2022, the following was added: Pandemic of 2020-2022

All of the above contribute to the situation of hopelessness among adults and become a contributing factor in the overall economic decline and increasing of the level of poverty among the residents of Appalachia. Loss of job opportunities leads to a greater stress level, leading to increased numbers of ACEs observed in the children growing up in this area of the United States. Unfortunately, these behaviors are not stagnant but reoccur in continuing generations, making them inter-generational. Values and cultural norms are being passed on from generation to generation, especially when children grow up living in close proximity to their older family members. Unfortunately, physical discipline, the influence of religion and the use of corporal punishment, and the need to maintain family privacy all continue to contribute to additional ACEs appearing in the responses to the questionnaire. Additional factors in the rise of responses to the ACEs are the following according to ORAU: geographic location (the Appalachian Trail known as GAME, Georgia to Maine); lack of community resources (churches, sports, community centers, counseling groups, social opportunities); poor health among adult caregivers (addiction); lack of appreciation and importance of education (lack of support from school groups, no intervention programs); lack of transportation; and a disregard for children living in Appalachia by outsiders. Most prevalent and with most impact were unemployment and "ruptured" attachments, death of an attachment figure.

ORAU also saw a "buffering" factor, some helpful solutions to ACEs, in these family living situations. Strong family cultural values and ties to their community help develop an appreciation for these values. Resiliency and identification of ACEs appearing in this study could be the keys to preventing the recurrence of ACEs in future generations. School-based therapy and intervention programs in the community are also needed, such as the Sanctuary program and Child Parent Psychotherapy (CPP). (Harris, 2018). Dr. Alicia Lieberman has designed this program of Child Parent Psychotherapy for birth to five (5) year olds and their parents based on the premise that addressing ACEs must be a team effort. (Harris, 2018) ORAU determined from their questionnaire results, that unemployment and ruptured attachment were the top two most critical and prevalent ACEs, with witnessing death, overdose, and repeated ruptures of relationships being the most harmful to the child.

In a survey of adults in 2017-2018 in *Child Trends*, the following was discovered: (excluding economic hardship) thirty percent (30%) of the adults surveyed reported one (1) ACE, fourteen percent (14%) reported two (2) or more ACEs. When economic hardships were included, forty-five percent (45%) reported experiencing one (1) or more. (A 2019 CDC study found that sixty percent (60%) of adults reported one ACE and more reported more than one. The CDC was convinced these numbers were inaccurate suspecting the reason for the lack of accuracy was due to self-reporting and honesty on the survey.)

The ORAU identified the following eight (8) areas of needed improvement discovered in their research. They are listed in order of their priority based on the research findings.

Community-based support, school-based support, education communication, home-based inter-generational support, lists of available resources, behavioral health professionals, transportation, substance abuse programs.

The Center for Disease Control and The Appalachian study

Contributing factors found by the CDC in the Appalachian Study included poverty, economic decline, value of privacy, drug addiction, cultural factors (acceptance of violence, influence of religion, and use of corporal discipline). A major factor found in this study was the ongoing epidemic of Opioid abuse. This situation continues today. A lack of community resources was also discovered leaving substance abusers, trauma victims and cultural issues unaddressed. *Education was not valued.*

A Lasting Effect Both Emotionally and Physically

Scenario #4

10 year old: Michael

Michael entered the picture when he was brought to the adolescent psychiatric department of a local hospital. He had been admitted for aggressive behavior against many of his classmates at a school dedicated to youth with emotional and behavioral problems. The staff at the school was familiar with students with these problems, but Michael was beyond what they could deal with in the classroom. Social services shared Michael's history in an effort to try to get him into a program to help with his anger management. His history revealed many ACEs issues beginning with his abandonment at age 2. He was found sitting on a street curb in only a diaper, having been left with a grandmother who was already overwhelmed with the custody of Michael's 2 older siblings in addition to other grandchildren. At age 3 he went into the foster care system. As he went from foster home to foster home, all of the ACEs he had been experiencing were discovered. He was the victim of both emotional and physical abuse. His household challenges were numerous, violence to his mother, substance abuse, mental illness, living in a single-parent household, and having a parent incarcerated. Neglect was the most evident of the ACEs, both emotional and physical. Michael suffered from lack of any attachment to a parental figure. Currently, as an adult Michael is still insecure in relationships but with the adoption a by family early in his teen years, he has learned to hold on to this stability he has found.

When assessing the neurologically-related effects caused by adverse

childhood experiences, four areas of concern must be addressed. How well can the child consistently perform according to his chronological age and his related developmental age? How well does he perform related to his physical development? How well does his physical and mental development correlate?

When determining an appropriate age of a child or adult for comparison purposes, use of an appropriate tool might be the Devereux Early Childhood Assessment-Infant (DECA-I), Devereux Early Childhood Assessment-Toddler (DECA-T), Devereux Early Childhood Assessment-Preschool Second Edition DECA-P2), and Devereux Adult Resilience Survey (DARS) to evaluate for resilience in the adult having experienced adverse experiences. The Devereux assessments evaluate attachment and relationships and self-regulation in children and relationships, internal beliefs, initiative, and self-control in adults.

Appearance and Affect of the Child Being Traumatized

Scenario #5

12 year old: Mark

Mark was a quiet boy who sat in the back of his sixth grade classroom. He came to school well dressed and clean. Through the morning he quietly watched and responded when questioned. After lunch break every day the other students complained about his odor. He would go to the school nurse who would call his father to take him home. Mark had diuresis, a serious medical condition. Fortunately, his classmates were compassionate. On further investigation it was discovered that his mother had passed away suddenly the previous summer. Mark's trauma was that he had lost his primary caregiver and therefore, unintended emotional neglect, although his father did his best. Mark had trouble coping with the daily stressors of school and had devised a way to escape by going home with the only person he could trust. Losing his mother cost him his self-esteem and gave him a hopeless feeling. Emotionally he was distraught and unable to express these feelings.

Looking at the child, how does his body perform in the following four (4) situations: Empathy, Emotional Response, Coordination and Movement, Heart Rate?

1. Empathy, Self-control and Literacy (Cortical response)

   Does the child have the ability to be empathic and is he able consistently demonstrate control over his actions? Does the traumatized child have the ability to express himself with the use appropriate vocabulary?

2. Emotional response (Limbic response)

   What kinds of emotional expressions does the child consistently use? Are they appropriate for his developmental age? Is the child able to monitor these emotional responses with regard to what others are doing?

3. Coordination and Movement (Midbrain response)

   Is the physical coordination and movement developmentally and age appropriate? (For example, is the child able to throw a ball, catch a ball, or ride a bicycle at the expected developmental age?)

4. Heart Rate: Fight, Flight, Freeze (Brainstem response)

   How well can the child monitor his heart rate to be able to determine whether to fight, run, or freeze in a threatening situation? Is his response consistent over time? Is the response reactionary with regard to the stimulus?

The evidence of affect and appearance on the growing child

Initially Adverse Experiences can start as early as while the fetus is still in utero. These experiences can affect the growing fetus and growing child while the lower parts of the brain continue to develop up until approximately two years of age. Empathy, self-control and the development of literacy start with the Cortical response. The young child begins to have feelings for others around him, show his feelings and start to develop spoken language (literacy). Between ages one (1) and four (4) both the Limbic system and the Midbrain are developing. The brain begins to organize, and the child is able to feel emotion and make connections with others around him. The developing Limbic system helps the child learn appropriate emotional responses to events happening to him. As the Midbrain grows, movement improves as the child begins to develop his ability to walk and move independently. Vision, hearing, pain, and sleep patterns develop at this point. As the Prefrontal Cortex continues to develop between age three (3) and six (6) years old, the child develops an ability to be empathetic, shows self-control and is beginning to develop more advanced literacy skills. As the brain organizes heart rate, breathing, blood pressure and swallowing, which are automatic responses, respond to Flight/Fight/Freeze in a traumatic situation.

Appropriate relationships are needed between the ages of one (1) and four (4) while the middle parts of the brain begin to organize and the child is able to feel emotion, physical pain, and begin learning to move and make connections with others around him. When any of these stages are compromised, disrupted development occurs. At this time, adverse experiences can exacerbate this disruption and delay the normal development of the child. Building attachment with an adult parent/caregiver at this point is critical as it is necessary for the basic needs to be provided to the child. If this attachment does not occur, the expectations of the child will become ones of rejection and harm. The result can be defensiveness and withdrawal, social distancing, and loneliness for the child.

Studying and Assessing Neurological Development

The first four (4) years of human development are the most critical time for brain development. This is also the time when trauma can do the most harm and have the greatest impact on the developing child. Underactivity in the Frontal Cortex is an indicator of abuse, with a significant difference in brain size. The brain is malleable and changeable as it continues to develop in the adolescent into his twenties (20's), with twenty-five (25) being the average age for full brain development.

For disrupted Neurodevelopment, the most rapid and significant time is up to four (4) years of age. Some of the most significant results are the decreased size of the corpus callosum, and as a result a decrease in performance of the motor, sensory and cognitive abilities. A common cause of disruption in this area of the brain is what is commonly known as shaken baby syndrome.

Social, emotional, cognitive impairment are evident with a life-long effect building from birth. Research using Magnetic Resonance Imaging (MRI) found nine (9) differences in areas of the brains of young adults who had experienced childhood abuse or trauma and those who did not. The areas with the most obvious changes were those effecting emotions and impulses. A decrease in the size of the hippocampus results in inability to learn and remember. These areas of decreased size and differences cause an inability to learn and remember and control emotions and behaviors, something that is obvious when the child begins formal education. These begin as simply as an inability to sit and participate in class appropriately and move on to more blatant negative behaviors, sometimes called "acting out".

Adoption of health-risk behaviors, usually seen at the beginning of adolescence, can result from overactivity of the amygdala and cause lack of ability to properly respond to stressful or dangerous activities. Other areas can affect motor skills, coordination, balance, and perception. During the time when the child should be able to do physical activities such as throw a ball and balance on a bike, he may be less able to accomplish these activities. His perception is also less accurate. He sees things through a distorted lens.

Disease, disability, and social problems can occur during early adolescence into adulthood. Behavior, emotions, and social functioning can be affected resulting in constant fearfulness, learning deficits, missing developmental milestones, and developing and maintaining interpersonal relationships. At this point the normally awkward adolescent is falling further behind from where he should be developmentally. His unaffected friends are moving past him as he matures more slowly. The results of this slower development are obvious, the affected child can become the object of bullying, further traumatization.

Early death can occur ten (10) to twenty (20) years prior to lifespan projections, taking into consideration culture, race, and ethnicity. This may be caused by disease or suicide through risky behaviors or drug involvement.

Length and intensity of the abuse must be considered. Treatment can be both physical and/or mental health and the duration and age of the child at the treatment onset is important. (Holmes, 2021) Young children who are removed from the traumatic situation early and placed in a therapeutic environment may have a greater success rate than those removed as pre-adolescents or adolescents.

Common symptoms found in children who have experienced ACEs use strong language, per Dr. Bruce Perry. Symptoms can be undiagnosable and unexplained or complex and consist of a combination of symptoms or paradoxical. Perhaps there is a side effect to medication or an extreme sensitivity to stimulants. The child may have difficulty with understanding "self" and relating experiences. There may be strong responses or malingering or imagined symptoms, and/or hypochondria. There may be highly activated responses or deep "freeze", a time of withdrawal. A threatened child may experience a precipitous onset of pain or an initially tolerated intervention with a declining later response. (Kain and Terrell, 2018)

The seven (7) areas of threat, thoughts, feelings and behavior, from calmness through alertness, alarm, fear, and finally terror. *(Activity in the brain stem: from Neocortex to Brain Stem.)* (Kain & Terrell, 2018)

Planning ability goes from an ability to plan long-term to a diminishing length of time for planning activities.

The child's *ability to think*, goes from abstract to looping thoughts, from concrete to reactionary.

His *hyperarousal* fight or flight from resting to aggressive, hypervigilant to defiant.

From *freezing to dissociative*, able to rest self to terror-causing loss of consciousness, avoidant to fetal rocking motion.

Cognitive awareness, regression from a minimal number of years to regression to infancy, eight to fifteen (8-15) years to one to three (1-3) year old behavior.

Response to interactions, ability to participate in discussions to non-verbal cues only, ability to talk through more reactive non-verbal cues.

Cognitive aptitude, normal intelligence quotient to forty (40) standard deviations below average one hundred (100). Stages drop ten (10) points from alert to alarm, to fear, ending in a potential loss of possibly sixty (60) points.

Depending on the developmental age of the child and the intensity and frequency of the adverse experiences, the above can cause extreme results in adolescence and adulthood. (Kain & Terrell, 2018)

Dr. Bruce Perry's 3Es come into play: Event, Experience, Effect. Event: how often, how old was the child, who was the perpetrator (abuser), how long did the experience last; experience: what was the severity, what interventions took place: and effect: what happened as a result of the event, was there an intervention provided by a caretaker, was there any therapy given to the subject. (SAMHSA)

Lasting Effects of Trauma

Scenario #6

14 year old: Joe

Joe attended school on an average of two (2) days each week. He could be seen standing at the end of the long road down to his house in the mornings that he attended, smoking a cigarette, while waiting for the school bus. Joe was quiet in class but just not involved in education. When his parents were contacted about his truancy, their only response was that he was needed to tend to animals at home. The state truancy office finally gave up on him. Joe's affect was one of quiet compliance. He was not a trouble-maker so that appeared to be okay with his parents. Joe was a victim of serious lack of concern for education, certainly a form of abuse and neglect, and poverty. Joe finally dropped out of school the beginning of high school. He appeared almost relieved when this happened as he had fallen so far behind he had no chance of graduating. He lived in a farm community and was able to work the family farm to survive. Joe was a victim of neglect, emotional and physical. It was a generational situation, where the parents fell into the same experiences as the children they were raising. Unfortunately, ACEs can be generational in all instances.

A child may have only one traumatic experience, but the type of this experience and its intensity can determine the overall outcome and length of the response. Perception, here again, is the key to whether or not the adverse experience is a brief event or lasting trauma. Does the child perceive that he was in a serious and/or chronic threat of continued danger. Take for instance, the global pandemic of 2020-2022. Depending on how this experience affected us, it was either a serious life-changing event or an event that caused some discomfort and mild stress or perhaps just an annoyance. Depending on our perception, we either dealt with it or let it become a serious traumatic event. For everyone it was unique to that particular person. Additionally, a major consideration is the developmental stage of the person experiencing the event. Is the person an adult, adolescent, or young child? Has the person experienced traumas before this time in his life or has the trauma been an ongoing experience? Places where children were watching the elders of their community die during the pandemic (2020-2022) had more impact than that of an adult experiencing the same thing. What should have been a somewhat normal progression of aging became traumatic for everyone in the family. Watching a loved one die from behind a glass window instead of by his bedside was traumatizing not only for children involved but for some adults. This was passed on inter-generationally among all family members.

The diagram below shows how ACEs can progress from childhood

trauma through Early Death, marking the steps between.

Mechanisms by which Adverse Childhood Experiences Influence Health and Wellbeing Throughout the Lifespan) Diagram #1

Taking a closer look into the resultant adolescent and adult long-term

effects of ACEs, more significance can be seen, from Traumatic Brain Injury

(TBIs), bone fractures and burns to decreased education, lower wage

occupation and lower personal and household income. Children suffering

ACEs may also experience mental health issues, risky behaviors (unplanned pregnancies, complications, and fetal death), cancer, diabetes, morbid obesity, heart disease and addiction. Without appropriate care, these impacts may be lasting causing early death, defined as death earlier than according to what is determined by actuarial science and the Bureau of Vital Statistics. Taking into consideration race, ethnicity, and nationality, the 2023 actuarial age projection is seventy-nine point eleven (79.11) years, a zero point eight percent (0.08%) increase from 2022. However, for each chronic disease, one point eight (1.8) years of life is subtracted from the seventy-nine point eleven (79.11) projected years. For instance, an adult reporting ten (10) ACEs can mean the loss of eighteen (18) years of life. Poverty is not only a result of childhood ACEs but can be an underlying cause for these adverse experiences called traumas.

Prior to adolescence, the impact can be seen as problematic behaviors in school. Children with ACEs are more likely to be suspended, put into detention, or otherwise removed from the classroom. Loss of time in the classroom can keep the child from progressing at the same rate as his peers. When the child falls behind, he looks to these removals from the classroom as a type of safety net, a means of protection from being seen as academically deficient. A safe environment with Trauma-Informed staff can help to deter problem behaviors and reinstate a calm atmosphere for learning. This approach also will resolve the issue of completed education. Students who are victims of ACEs but have a nurturing learning atmosphere, will remain in school to complete their education thus removing the stigma of poverty and the resulting job insecurity.

Depression, anxiety, and Post-Traumatic-Stress-Disorder (PTSD) can appear in early adolescence. Sexual activity in early adolescence can produce dangerous and unwanted pregnancy. Young girls are more likely to deliver their babies prematurely, under the normal birth weight, or stillborn. These infants once born, can be unviable and often unwanted. Many times, the mother's education is curtailed putting her into the category of low-wage earner or unemployed. Unsafe sexual activity can also result in sexually transmitted diseases, Acquired Immunodeficiency Syndrome (AIDs) and Human Immunodeficiency Virus (HIV), life-long diseases for these children continuing into adulthood. Diseases from cancer, diabetes, heart disease and obesity to depression can result in life-long physical and mental health issues. Alcoholism and drug use can occur and cause health issues leading to an early mortality. The result for the child is further delay in or absence of his education and result in lower income jobs and poverty. All these impacts to the child are lasting.

Looking at the diagram below, Injury, Mental health, Maternal health, Infectious Disease, Chronic Disease, Risky Behaviors and Lost Educational and Job Opportunities continue to accumulate to make a disastrous future for the child who has adverse experiences early in life. The victim goes from injury inflicted by another person to such a loss of self, he continues the process causing the injury to himself. It is critical that ACEs be treated and a program to abort any further outbreaks. Further studies must be implemented to view in a longitudinal perspective the best ways to reach children trapped in this stigma.

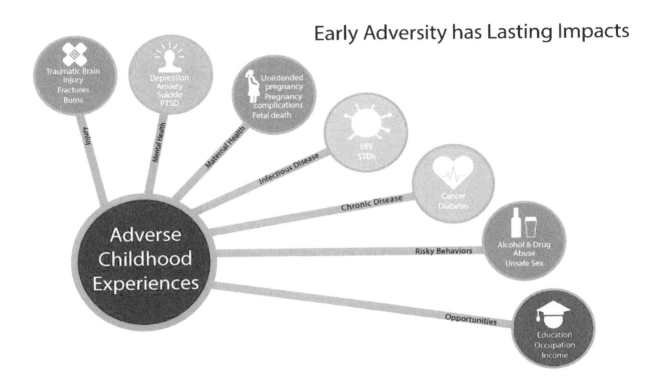

Approaches to better enable learning for victims of trauma Diagram #2

Understanding the role that psychological trauma plays in child

development is the first step to helping the child. What is the

developmental stage of the child? What are the ACEs affecting the child?

Looking again at the 3E's, *event, experience, effects*? What age is the child?

What are the effects the child is demonstrating from the exposure to ACEs?

Where is the child in relation to Perry's 4R's, *regulate, relate, reason,*

reflect? Where can treatment begin with Trauma-informed Care?

Explaining the role and impact adverse childhood experiences have on mental, physical, and socioemotional health in reversing ACEs is the first step. Looking at the pyramid of debilitating health issues can assist in identifying the impact to each individual child. Identifying factors that promote resilience in children's development is important. Adding Trauma-Informed care is a necessary addition to the developmental agenda for any child who is a victim of ACEs.

Discussing ways to integrate a trauma-informed approach into areas in which children are treated and cared for, including families, education, community resources and health care must be explored. A community resource group containing advocacy personnel, teachers, church leaders, and community leadership must be developed to address the needs of children and their families to live ACE-free. Free training for all personnel and volunteers in Trauma-Informed Care must be provided.

Culture is an important issue and impacts an individual's exposure to, understanding of, and response to trauma over a lifespan. A close study of cultural impacts that affect children must be viewed to determine where

ACEs are a part of the problem or resolution.

Using Trauma-Informed Care for Recovery from Adverse Childhood Experiences

Scenario #7

15 year old: Jim

Jim was a high school sophomore with a good attendance and GPA record. Very suddenly, Jim began having severe stomach pains preventing him from attending school on a regular basis. His concerned parents took him to a variety of doctors for a diagnosis, but nothing helped. This went on for two years, with his school sending home assignments. At the end of his junior year, the thought of college seemed to get Jim back into the classroom. Jim's trauma was twofold. His parents divorced and his older siblings went off to college. He lost his same-sex role model, who moved away and both siblings he depended on went to college out of state. Jim's trauma, although unintentional, caused him to feel isolated and stressed. This emotional neglect was exacerbated by his mother having to go to work full time and survive on an income much less than he was used to having. Jim succeeded in finishing high school and moving on to college. Some of the emotions followed him from his trauma, but therapy helped to stabilize his feelings.

Adverse Childhood Experiences (ACEs) are a national public health problem

affecting countless American citizens. An accurate count is difficult because

all of the published surveys are self-reporting. Vocabulary such as

"prevalence" and "more likely than not" is used to identify victims of adverse experiences in a report from the Buffalo Center for Social Research.

A suggested program for those affected and as a resolution to the

continuance of ACEs is Trauma-Informed Care (TIC). According to the

Buffalo Center for Social Research, there are five (5) guiding values and

principles that can provide healing and recovery for traumatized

individuals. These are: Safety: with respected private and common areas

regarding physical and emotional safety for the client; Choice: rights and

responsibilities are detailed and clients are given choice and control over

these choices; Collaboration: clients are given a role of power in making

decisions in planning and evaluation of their choices; Trustworthiness:

respectful boundaries are set to ensure clarity, and boundaries;

Empowerment: clients will feel empowered and validated by the agency

and staff. (SAMHSA) When addressing the needs of a client, it is safer to

assume that this person is a victim than not as it is more likely a correct

assumption. TIC addresses complex trauma with its accompanying life-

changing toxic stress. The Crisis Prevention Institute adds: Peer Support to

enhance collaboration and share lived experiences.

Some trauma experiences go beyond conscious memory and affect behavior, relationships, and attitudes. With trauma, the victim sees everything through a lens of fear and chronic threat. They are in a constant state of hyperarousal, easily startled, have difficulty staying focused, and feels constant guilt or blame. They have lost a desire for pleasurable activities. For these reasons, we must meet the subject where they are with acceptance and empathy, helping the client to feel safe. Building trust and helping clients to share with others is critical. The client must be empowered to be a critical part of their own recovery and be engaged with the professionals around him. Finally, acknowledgement of the client's cultural and gender issues, if any, must be recognized and understood. Many times these very issues are the ones that brought the client to this place of being traumatized and as a victim of adverse experiences. TIC is not a one-size-fits-all but is a treatment plan that is individualized for each client. (Cleveland Clinic, 2022)

Using Trauma-Informed Care For Treatment, What happened to you?

Scenario #8

14 year old: Ann

Ann was a straight "A" student, but quiet and reserved in class. She was always ready for class and never gave anyone of the staff any trouble. Friday was test day in her Social Studies class. One particular Friday her behavior was unusual. When the teacher investigated, Ann had her textbook open inside her desk, obviously cheating. As was the teacher's protocol, her test paper was taken, marked with a "0" and sent home for a signature. As this unusual behavior was investigated, it was discovered that Ann was disciplined for grades below an "A" and she had not studied for the test. There might not have been any physical abuse, but certainly emotional abuse. Her parents kept their children clean and fed as best they could. Finances were a concern for the family. Education was important to them, and they expected their children to succeed, not an indication of ACEs. Her only route to college would be a scholarship. "Disciplined" can fall into emotional abuse, if perceived by the child as a reason to break rules. She later earned a scholarship to an elite university and continued communicating with her former teachers. Was she the victim of unusual discipline or too great a regard for education? Sometimes ACEs works both ways.

No matter whether trauma was long-lasting or a single event, Trauma-Informed Care is important for recovery. Trauma changes the perspective of the person. Trauma-Informed Care can be defined as a means of thinking and practical interventions that are used to understand the extreme trauma that holds an individual mentally, physically, and emotionally. (Crisis Recourse Guide) Triggers or stimuli can be real or imagined, depending on the person's perception. Triggers can leave emotional, physiological, or behavioral responses, fight, flight or freeze. Trauma can be acute, a single event; chronic, extended exposure; or complex, single event that has long-lasting effects. (Resource Guide) Traumatization happens when the child or adult does not have adequate internal or external resources for coping with the trigger or stimulation. (Resource Guide)

Seven (7) ideas for preventing re-traumatizing.

1.   Collect data about client's behavior and responses

2.   Learn to read the client's behavior

3.   Watch for obvious negative behaviors

4.   Focus on what the client can-do not as a victim

5.   Meet client where they are

6.   Weigh appropriateness of physical interventions

7.   Debrief after a crisis with not only the client but colleagues after an

interaction

The Four R's of Trauma-Informed Care according to the Agency for

Healthcare and Quality are:

REALIZE

Understand both the prevalence of events and impact of trauma on

the individual needing help.

RECOGNIZE

See the signs and symptoms of trauma in people.

RESPOND

Bring together knowledge, practice, procedures, and policies to

address the trauma in clients.

RESIST RETRAUMATIZING

Actively protect clients building clinical and organizational changes to

support the safety and recovery for traumatized children,

adolescents, and adults.

(Agency for Healthcare Research and Quality)

Developing resilience in the child or adolescent is a critical part of TIC,

remembering that perception is important to resilience. A determination of

whether the experience is traumatic or more of a learning experience is

critical to how the issue is addressed. The APA defines resilience as *"the*

process and outcome of successfully adapting to difficult or challenging life

experiences, especially through mental, emotional, and behavioral flexibility

and adjustment to external demands." (APA) *Psychology Today* defines

resilience in a briefer statement, the *"ability to recover stronger or at least*

as strong as before the experience", through developing a positive attitude,

optimism, regulated emotions, and the ability to see failure as helpful.

Regardless of where we get a definition, TIC begins with helping children,

adolescents, and adults going through ACEs recovery to overcome the trauma and become resilient. Regulating their emotions and facing the adversity can be taught. Clinicians and educators can help in this recovery process by teaching that adversity can be overcome.

Dr. Martin Seligman, of the University of Pennsylvania, has been a key researcher of optimism. In his book, *Learned Optimism, How to Change Your Mind and Your Life,* he describes two (2) models for working with traumatized children, the ABC model and the ABCDE model. Utilizing the ABC model, the parent or other adult will design an adverse (A) situation, relating it to the child. The child will then give a Brief (B) answer as to why this may have happened to him. He then follows with what he believes the Consequence (C) or action taken might be. At this point the adult leads the child into a discussion of why he feels the way he does. The adult is helping the child to go from a negative (pessimistic) feeling to building a more positive (optimistic) response. In other words, the child will be led to see or perceive the situation differently. After using this format, the child should be moving to more positive thinking about his own adversities. Once the child has understood the process of ABC, the adult can move on to ABCDE.

This model adds two (2) more aspects to the exercise. Once the child has related the Consequences, the child will be asked to Dispute these ideas. Thoughts are not always accurate, and their accuracy may be disputed. Is the situation really as he has perceived it to be? He has now worked his way into Energization, where he can look at the Adversity and see it for what it may actually be, less traumatic than it originally appeared. (Seligman, 2006) Once again we can see where perception is a factor in how much an adverse experience may affect a child, and how using therapies can assist in changing how the child views things.

Using Trauma-Informed Care for Prevention in Victims of ACEs

All of the above techniques can be taught in clinicians offices, community centers, classrooms and such to assist in the prevention of ACEs. Add to this adaptation a better view of the world and engagement in it, more and better resources made available, and educating coping strategies to both children and their parents.

"Resilience" appears in all literature relating to ACEs and childhood recovery and prevention. Dr. Norman Garmezy states that it is only when a person is faced with adversity that it can be determined if they are resilient. Does the person succeed in going past the adversity or does he let it traumatize him? Garmezy says it depends on the "intensity and duration" of the experience. In Garmezy's pioneering study he identified "resilience" as the key to whether or not the person was able to overcome difficult circumstances. He found that some children in spite of their household challenges, were able to succeed in life and school. (Konnikova, 2016)

Dr. Emmy Warner found the same result, if children were resilient, they could succeed. In fact, she found when measuring their "locus of control", they had the ability to achieve beyond their expected circumstances. They were better than two (2) standard deviations above the standardized group. Werner, looking at resilience, found that it can also change over time. Sometimes stressors become so overwhelming that they overcome the resilience the child has developed. Others, who did not show any resilience, are able to develop resilience as they aged. (Konnikova, 2018)

Dr. George Bonanno asks the question, if all humans had the same fundamental stress response, "why do some people use (resilience) so much more frequently or effectively than others?" His studies revealed that perception was evident. Humans create events in our minds, building the observation of an event. In other words, humans create adversity from events that can be stressful and traumatic or not, depending on how they perceive them. Bonanno's research focused on primarily harmful and negative events, Potentially Traumatic Event (PTE). According to his epidemiological data, Bonanno sees stressful or traumatic events not as a reason for problematic later functioning in adults, unless it is perceived as traumatic. (Konnikova, 2016)

Kevin Ochsner, a neuroscientist at Columbia University, believes that resilience can be taught. When we think of something, instead of thinking negatively, put the experience or event in positive terms. He believes this can be a permanent fix. (Konnikova, 2018)

Dr. Martin Seligman, University of Pennsylvania psychologist, has been a pioneer in the field of positive psychology. He explains that thoughts should be changed from internal to external, bad things are not my fault; and changing from global ideas to specific, moving ideas from a large scale to small; and permanent to impermanent, can be a fix for negative thought patterns. The idea in Garmezy of "locus of control" or changing from external to internal also appears in Seligman's work. (Konnikova, 2018) Resilience can be taught and retained, especially for children, adolescents, and adults who have become victims of adverse childhood experiences.

As human beings, we constantly are exaggerating events. We worry and make more out of an event then there is, by "ruminating" (Konnikova) until it has become a major challenge with which we are unable to deal. If we attempt to learn resilience, what needs to be done, according to these psychologists, is to put the experience into perspective, move on, and learn from the experience. (Konnikova, 2016)

The Center for Disease Control and Violence Prevention gives six (6) strategies for ACE prevention. They fall into the following categories: economic, social, children's early education, skills development, youth to adult interactions, and long terms issues.

To address each of these: economic issues through developing financial security and family-centered work environments; social: improved education, a fair justice system, and joining men and boys in alliance for prevention against violence. Early childhood education through home interventions, high quality care, and family-centered preschool. Applying skill training through relationship building, teaching parenting skills, and social-emotional learning. Connecting youth to appropriate caregivers

through mentoring and afterschool programs. To lessen or eliminate long-

term effects of ACEs through victim-centered, and family-centered

treatment and prevention of ACEs and prevent problem behaviors and

substance abuse. All of these can be initiated and supported through

communities and trained volunteers.

Education, School Systems and Clinicians Help Resolve the ACEs Problem

Dr. Bruce Perry states: "Education is a brain-based activity, and a fundamental task of education is to change the brain." If we were to look at students now who have not been inside a classroom due the pandemic, what, if any, changes would we see? How many of these brain-developed responses would be evident in a Functional Behavioral Assessment, for example? How would we answer the question "What happened to you?" or as one father of four stated: "Change: Why is this happening to me?" to "What is this trying to teach me?

Studying the theories of learning and cognitive development of the child, educational psychologist Dr. Jerome Bruner sees the same characteristics as many of the other educators. For instance, children must be active learners and the content be intellectually appropriate for the child. Further, content can be taught to the child in stages that the child is prepared to learn the content. According to Bruner, "the aim of education should be to create autonomous learners (learning to learn)." (Mcleod, 2023) Language is a key to learning as well, enabling the child to be able to give responses. What about the child in the classroom who has been traumatized and is not appropriately prepared to learn? Or the child behind in language development? This child is not able to develop the problem-solving skills necessary to learn from a series of learning situations.

In the 1960's Bruner explained his "spiral curriculum", a means of gradually increasing the difficulty of the levels of the subjects. He theorized that children learn more from doing than seeing or hearing. He called this "Discovery Learning". Utilizing simplifying tasks, encouraging and motivating, showing models of expectations, and presenting important tasks, the child can be motivated to learn on his own. (Mcleod) Putting all of this into a Trauma-Informed environment can encourage the child suffering from adverse experiences to begin to trust those around him.

Professionals using Trauma-Informed Care look at some psychological approaches. Educators who use a cognitive approach look at how students approach learning. Is the student enthusiastic or unable to get involved? Is lack of involvement due to a lack of progress in learning the subject matter?

The constructivist and experientialist look at the social and cultural and

experiences the child has had as influences. Are ACEs (Adverse Childhood

Experiences) a factor? Teachers in the classroom play an important part in

how the child recovers from adverse experiences and responds to Trauma-

Informed Care.

Dr. Bruce Perry's Neurosequential model: Regulate, Relate, Reason,

Reflect

Regulate (self-control of behavior)

By the time a child has spent some time in kindergarten, he should be able

to monitor and control his behavior in the classroom. For this reason,

Regulation is the first step in the Neurosequential Model. The child who

cannot regulate will have behavioral difficulties at this first level and

consequently as he moves on to more complex steps. Regulation is not

something that comes naturally but is taught. Teachers with Trauma-

Informed practice are able to lead young (5-6) year olds into the practice of implementing Regulation. Especially if they have not had the opportunity to learn this in their home. Children who are in homes where ACEs are common may not have the opportunity to learn prior to entering school.

Relate (brain activity to behavior)

As the child matures, he is more able to relate his behavior to what his brain is telling him to do. This relation of brain activity to physical behavior is critical to the maturation of the child and his ability to relate to others around him. Knowing right from wrong is the basis for this part of the 4R's. When a child enters school knowing what the right thing is to do and what is not, he is on his way to a successful educational experience. The child who has grown up being a victim to ACEs has not had the opportunity to learn. The correct thing to do is far from being what he has experienced. He has been trained to respond to abuse and fight, run, or fear.

Reason (determine a cause for these thoughts and resulting behavior)

Stepping into the Reasoning mode, the child is able to not only relate thoughts to behavior, but to understand the why behind his thoughts. He can judge the causes for his behavior, although he may not completely understand how to make changes. At this point the child should be able to understand why he is doing the things he is. But the child who has been in a home with abuse only sees the results of abuse and how he must respond in order to save himself. He doesn't understand the why of the abuse he receives. A safe environment with Trauma-Informed care will help to change this behavior.

Reflect (study conclusions, develop a strategy)

At this stage, the brain begins to organize, and the child is able to feel emotion and make connections with others around him. At this point, the child can take a good look at the challenging and often confusing behavior he is demonstrating, self-determine its cause and help to either continue the behavior or stop it if it is detrimental to his wellbeing. He can say "this works" or "this does not work" for me. This is not always a given for the child who has grown up with ACEs. Studying his own behavior and coming to conclusions about it may be easier than learning strategies for change.

Once again, being guided by someone who is trained in Trauma-Informed Care will be able to lead the child into a reflective mode. (Perry)

The Neurosequential Model (4R's) aligns well with Seligman's ABC and ABCDE Models. Implementing them together builds a strong Trauma-Informed program for the classroom.

Looking at what determines whether a child will have a positive outcome from TIC, the most common factor is having a relationship with a stable parent or caregiver. This relationship can help the child build abilities in emotional control and positive experiences. Helping the child develop a sense of self-worth helps him to build resilience. When given an opportunity to self-regulate he will develop more self-assurance. Having cultural traditions to connect with help to ensure the building of resilience. Since not all stress is negative, anticipating a holiday or vacation for instance, and the child should be able to differentiate between this positive and negative stress. Positive stress can teach the child to learn coping strategies, where negative stress can be a learning tool as well depending on perception. Coping strategies can be learned at any age, childhood

through adulthood. These strategies to develop resilience can help to

manage behaviors for both children suffering from ACEs and adults

managing health issues.

The Covid Factor and How It Exacerbated the Effects of Trauma

Interviews with 4ᵗʰ Grade Students:

The following information was gathered from nine (9) year old, fourth (4ᵗʰ) grades students in New Bern, North Carolina in a video provided by the National Assessment Governing Board (NAGB) on their website. The following were the four (4) questions asked and answered by the children in their own words.

How did the Pandemic, Covid, change your learning?

➢ Struggled learning on my own, prefer *school in person*.

➢ Missed the *social aspect*, missed my friends.

What was the hardest thing?

➢ Having working parents and needing help with schoolwork when parents were at work.

➢ Distractions at home.

What is good about the current school year? (Post-Pandemic)

- It's great to *make new friends.*

- Reading is improving, my teacher is helping me learn to read better.

- It's good to be *back with my old friends.*

- Doing *"group work"* in class is easier than doing it alone

- Ability to *communicate with the teacher in person.*

What do you like about school?

- Teachers "push you to be your best."

- You have *help* pushing through difficult times and situations.

- I like everything!

Notice all the references (in italics) of students feeling social isolation, a common result of ACEs. The pandemic, although not a man-made or natural disaster, had the same effect on children.

Lower Academic Assessment Scores

According to recent National Assessment of Educational Progress (NAEP) reports, standardized achievement scores for fourth (4th) grade students in reading and math have declined dramatically. A special administration of

reading and mathematics assessments in 2022 showed an average decline
of five (5) points in reading and seven (7) points in mathematics over the
average scores for nine (9) year old students in 2020. This decline became
the greatest in reading since 1990 and the first decline ever in
mathematics. The lower the percentile placement of the student, the
greater the decline in both reading and mathematics. All of these percentile
declines were in the statistically significant category. Students with
disabilities showed only a significant decrease in reading scores. Seventy
percent (70%) of the children taking the 2022 NAEP assessment said in an
interview that they had remote learning during the Pandemic. The majority
of these students who were higher-performing students had access to
computers, high-speed internet, quiet place to work, had a teacher
available, and someone to help with schoolwork, where lower-performing
children did not appear to have access to these. An additional area for the
higher-performing students was their ability to determine when they
needed help, ask for it or knew how to access the information online.

➤

natural disaster, had the same effect on children. (Reference pages 8 and 14-15)

If we look at Dr. Bruce Perry's Neurosequential model for education and also consider the fact that for almost three (3) years students did not have the benefit of learning from a certified education professional in a classroom, is there any reason not to expect these kinds of results? Keep in mind that learning to read and do mathematics begins in grades one (1) to three (3) primarily. This is when children *learn to read* so that when they reach fourth (4th) grade and upwards, they are able to *read to learn*, making sense of the words and using contextual clues. The fourth (4th) grade students quoted from the NSGB video, pages eighty-seven to eight-nine (87-89), were in this category of reading to learn. If we look at educational approaches for children who are victims of trauma, we see many of these occur outside of the home. Taking a four (4) year old who has suffered from one (1) or more of these traumatic ACEs events and putting him in a nurturing environment can begin to start building the resilience needed to counteract the long-term effects and make academic learning a successful activity. Building this resilience is an exercise in brain-changing activity, however, understanding how to approach this exercise must come first.

Looking at the older student, middle or high school age, and his response to the Covid pandemic, we see a difference from the younger student. Where the younger student has not had the school-related experience for as long as the older student, he may still not be thriving as he should, but the older student has been denied the classroom experience and missed both content and a sharing experience.

What are teachers looking for when they stand in front of a classroom? Are they seeing the young student who has experienced ACEs? Having given an informal survey to my college classes, I have found that no one has been totally eliminated from all ACEs. Each has experienced at least one traumatic experience. Are teachers able to design a program that will encourage ALL students in the class to participate? Are they being culturally aware? Whether in a college face-to-face or online class where no one has been in a face-to-face situation in almost three years or in a Kindergarten through twelfth grade class in the same situation, there are students returning to an unfamiliar situation. Should we be expecting them to achieve the same results they were achieving prior to experiencing any traumatic event? What do our students look like? Are they clean, freshly showered? Are their clothes clean and do have enough clothes to wear? These are obvious signs of neglect, poverty, and other signs of the presence of ACEs. The child who is being bullied for the way he/she looks is not able to learn.

How can we use Trauma-Informed Care in everyday life? Realizing that ACEs are so prevalent and impactful on our society as to become a major public health issue, should bring this issue to the attention of everyone in our communities. When we look at the issue, we can see the results of trauma in the homelessness and crime in our neighborhoods. These signs should make it evident that we have a major social issue to contend with to rid our streets of violence and poverty. How are we, as a nation, responding to what is not going unnoticed in our cities, towns, and neighborhoods. In an attempt to refrain from retraumatizing individuals we are not addressing the issue. Screening for children suffering from ACEs should be a priority. Learning about our bias and how it affects how we live with others and our role in improving the environment for children suffering from adverse experiences. Learning about our experiences working with the effects of ACEs on children should be a priority. Finally, knowing how to communicate what we know with parents, family and caretakers of children with adverse experiences is critical. (Crisis Prevention Institute)

Scenarios

While reading the included scenarios, please think about ACEs and TIC. How would you approach each one of these situations using what you now know about ACEs and TIC information? Each one of these real-life scenarios demonstrates how an adverse experience(s) can traumatize a child, whether still young or moving into adolescence. Children learn to adapt to the environment they find themselves in at the time, whether it be traumatic or not, as these scenarios demonstrate.

These are all scenarios that have been experienced by this author. Names are all pseudonyms.

References

1. About the CDC-Kaiser ACE Study. ACE Pyramid
   https://www.cdc.gov/violenceprevention/aces/bout.html

2. ACES and Toxic Stress: Frequently Asked Questions. Center on the Developing Child Harvard University.
https://developingchild.harvard.edu/resources/aces-and-toxic-stress-frequently-asked/questions/

3.Adverse Childhood Experiences section of the Violence Prevention Branch of the CDC
https://www.cdc.gov./violenceprevention/aces/index.html

4.Adverse Childhood Experiences. (2022)
https://www.ncsl.org/health/adversechildhood-experiences

5.Agency for Healthcare Research and Quality. *Trauma-Informed Care.* https://www.ahrq.gov/ncepcr/tools/fact-sheets/trauma.html

6.Boschma, J., Merrill, C., Murphy-Texidor, J. (CNN) Mass Shootings in the US. https://www.cnn.com/2023/01/24/us/mass-shootings-fast-facts/index.html

7.Cherry, K (2022) *What is Educational Psychology?* Verywell Mind. Https://www.verywellmind.com/what-is-educational-psychology-2795157?print

8. Donovan, SE (1998) *Assessing The Effectiveness of a Charter School Program for At-Risk Students.* A dissertation submitted to the faculty of Wilmington College in partial fulfillment of the requirements for Doctor of Education in Innovation and Leadership.

9."Exploring Adverse Childhood Experiences in Appalachia, A summary of Findings". Oak Ridge Associated Universities, Appalachian Regional Commission, and the Centers for Disease Control and Prevention. (2018) https://www.orau.gov/hsc/downloads/RuralSummitForChildhoodSuccess/ACEs%20in%20Appalachia_Summary%20Report_FINAL_pdf

10."Exploring Adverse Childhood Experiences in Appalachia". File:///D:/ACEs%20in%20Appalachia_Summary_%20Report_FINAL.pdf

11.Fast Facts. CDC Control and Prevention. Preventing Adverse Childhood Experiences. www.cdc.gov/violenceprevention/aces/fastfacts.html

12. Felitti, V.J., et al. (1998) American Journal of Preventative Medicine. "Relationship of Childhood Abuse and Household Dysfunction to Many of the Leading Causes of Death in Adults. The Adverse Childhood Experience (ACE) Study. https://www.ajpmonline.org/article/S0749-3797(98)00017-8/fulltext#back-B1B2

13. Gun Violence Archive. https://www.gunviolencearchive.org/reports

14. Giano, Z, Weeler, D.L., Hubach, R.D. (2020) The Frequencies and Disparities of Adverse Childhood Experiences in the U.S. BMC Public Health

15. Harris, N.B. 2018. *The Deepest Well, Healing the Long-Term Effects of Childhood Trauma.* Mariner Books. Com

16. Hege, A., et al. "Characteristics of Respondents and ACEs Within Appalachia and Outside Appalachia". https://www.researchgate.net/figure/characteristics-of-respondents-and-ACEs-within-Appalachia-and-outside-Appalachia-North_tb12_321943048

17. Holmes, L (2021) "How Emotional Abuse in Childhood Changes the Brain". https://www.verywellmind.com/childhood-abuse-changes-the-brain

18. How Racism Can Affect Child Development". Center on the Developing Child, Harvard University. https://developingchild.harvard.edu/resources/racism-and-ecd/

19. Kain, K.L. & Terrell, S.J. (2018) *Nurturing Resilience: Helping Clients Move Forward from Developmental Trauma.* North Atlantic Books, Berkley, CA.

20. Konnikova, M. (2016) "How People Learn To Become Resilient". https://www.newyorker.com/science/maria-konnikova/the-secret-formula-for-resilience/

21. Maul, A. (2017) State and Federal Support of Trauma-Informed Care: Sustaining the Momentum. Center for Health Care Strategies. https://www.chcs.org/state-federal-support-trauma-informed-care-sustaining-momentum/

22. McLean, S (2018) "Developmental differences in children who *have* experienced adversity".

https://www.aifs.gov.au/resources/practices-guides/developmental-differences-children-who-have-experienced-adversity

23.McLeod, S (2023) "Bruner's Theory of Learning and Cognitive Development". Simply Psychology. 2023
https://www.simplypsychology.org/bruner.html

24.Murthy, V. (2020) *Together*. HarperCollins Publishers, Inc. New York, NY

25.National Assessment Governing Board, website. NAEP, Nation's Report Card. https://www.nagb.gov/naep-subject-areas/long-term-trend.html

26.National Conference of State Legislatures. "Adverse Childhood Experiences" https://www.ncsl.org/research/health/adverse-childhood-experiences-aces.aspx

27.Neurosequential Model in Education (NME), classroom-based approach. Dr. Bruce Perry.

28.Perry, B.D. (2013) "Brief Reflections on Childhood, Trauma, and Society". The ChildTrauma Academy Press, Houston, TX

29.Perry, B.D. Neurosequential Model of Therapeutics, Brain Development (Neurosequential.com)

30.Perry, B.D. (2021) *What Happened To You? Conversations on Trauma, Resilience, and Healing.* Melcher Media, New York

31.Poole, N & Greaves, L (ed). 2012. "Becoming Trauma Informed". Center for addiction and mental health. Camh.

32."Resilience". Center on the Developing Child, Harvard University. https://developingchild.harvard.edu/resources/inbrief-resilience-series/

33."Resilience is Important for Children And Adults". Https://centerforresilientchildren.org/home/about-resilience/

34.Ryan, C (2020) "Calming the body before calming the mind: Sensory strategies for children affected by trauma". https://www.aifs.gov.au/resources/short-articles/calming-body-calming-mind-sensory-strategies-children-affected-trauma/

35.Substance Abuse and Mental Health Services https://www.samhsa.gov

36."Trauma-Informed Care". Agency for Healthcare Research and Quality. https://www.ahrq.gov/ncepcr/tools/fact-sheets/trauma.html

37. "Trauma-Informed Care, Resource Guide".
https://www.crisisprevention.com

38. "What Are ACEs? And How Do They Relate to Toxic Stress?"
https://developingchild.harvard.edu/resources/aces-and-toxic-stress-frequently-asked-questions/

39. "What is Trauma-Informed Care?" University of Buffalo. Buffalo Center for Social Research. https://social/work.buffalo.edu/social-research/institutes-centers/institute-on-trauma-informed-care/what-is-trauma-informed-care.html

40. Wikipedia Mass Shooting in the United States.
https://en.wikipedia.org/wiki/List_of_mass_shootings_in_the_United_States_in_2021

41. "Why Trauma-Informed Care Matters". Cleveland Clinic/Mental Health, August 11,2022
https://www.health.clevelandclinic.org/trauma-informed-care/

42. Wellpoint Mental Health Services
https://www.Wellpoint.org/services/mental-health/neurosequential-model-therapeutics-hmt/

Dr. Suzanne Donovan was born and raised in Pennsylvania. She has her undergraduate degree in English from Moravian College (now University), Bethlehem, PA; her Masters in Education degree from Chestnut Hill College in Philadelphia; and her Doctorate from Wilmington College (now University). Her education experience ranges from a classroom teacher and administrator to facilities for students with Behavioral and Developmental issues in Special Needs settings. In addition she has been a Charter School developer and creator in both Delaware and other states and countries. She continues to teach as a Professor of Psychology on the university level.

She lives in Southern Delaware with her husband and 3dogs. She is a Mom, Grandmom, and Great-Grand-Mom. Her hobbies center around her family and time on the beach reading.

Made in the USA
Columbia, SC
20 October 2024

44769532R00059